This Is How _I KETO_

Low-Carb Recipes for Your Lifestyle

By: Sonia Camis

Cover Illustration By: Ruthie Pagan

ISBN 978-1-0914-4960-2

MY DEDICATION

I dedicate this book first to Jesus Christ, my Lord and Savior. Without you, Lord, I would not be who I am or where I am today. Thank you, Jesus, for being who you are.

To my best friend, confidant and my everything, Frankie. You are an amazing man. You are an amazing husband and father. You work so hard to ensure that our family is taken care of in all aspects. You were created just for me!
I love you forever,
Your Wife

To my boys. My monkey's. You are the reason I am a mom. I strive to be better in every area of my life so that I may set a standard and example for you guys. I am here for you. Always remember, put God first and everything else will follow.

Love you,
Mami

FIND WHAT YOU CRAVE – TABLE OF CONTENTS

MAIN DISH

Air Fryer
Buttermilk Fried Chicken Breasts

"If Almond flour is NOT your thing, you have options. You can use Coconut Flour or Whey Protein. Be sure to check the carbs first! This Recipe works great with bone-in chicken as well."

—SoniaLee

Recipe Serves

8 Servings

Ingredients	Amount	
Chicken Breasts, boneless, skinless cutlets	3	lb
Heavy Whipping Cream	1	cup
Organic Apple Cider Vinegar with the mother	1	tbsp
Spicy Brown Mustard	1/4	cup
Dried Basil	1	tbsp
Dried Parsley	1	tbsp
Black Pepper	1	tsp
Sugar Free Maple Syrup	2	tbsp
Cayenne Pepper	1	tsp
Pink Himalayan Salt	2	tbsp
Almond Flour (or Coconut Flour or Whey Protein)	3	cup

Nutrition Facts

Servings: 8

Amount per serving

Calories	311
	% Daily Value*
Total Fat 13.1g	17%
Saturated Fat 3.8g	19%
Cholesterol 119mg	40%
Sodium 1953mg	85%
Total Carbohydrate 6g	2%
Dietary Fiber 1.5g	6%
Total Sugars 0.4g	
Protein 42.1g	
Calcium	3%
Iron	9%
Potassium 32mg	1%

*The % Daily Value (DV) tells you how much a nutrient in a food serving contributes to a daily diet. 2,000 calorie a day is used for general nutrition advice.

Instructions –Buttermilk

1. In a small bowl combine the apple cider vinegar and the heavy whipping cream.
2. Allow them to get to know each other for at least 10 minutes.
3. Stir well and set aside.

Instructions — Chicken

1. In a large bowl combine the following: buttermilk, mustard, basil, parsley, maple syrup, 1 teaspoon of salt and black pepper. Stir until well combined.
2. Add the chicken breasts and make sure they are coated on all sides.
3. Refrigerate for 4 hours, or better yet, overnight. ***Before cooking, allow the chicken to come to room temperature.
4. In a separate bowl combine the following: almond flour, cayenne pepper and 2 tablespoons of salt. Stir until well combined and set aside.
5. Dip the chicken into the dry mixture until all sides are well coated and transfer to a deep dish.
6. Allow these to sit for 10 minutes and then dip them into the dry mixture again.
7. Now you are ready to cook these bad boys!
8. Transfer these to your air fryer. Cook for 15 minutes at 400*F.
9. Turn them and cook them for another 7-10 minutes at 400*F. Or until they are browned to your liking.

Notes _____

_____

_____

_____

Air Fryer – Chicken Chicharrones "Chicharrones de Pollo"

**"This is amazing with my Brussels & bacon recipe!"
—SoniaLee**

Mona Khalid —
"Hi Lee Love all your recipes"

Nutrition Facts

Servings: 8	
Amount per serving	
Calories	**237**
	% Daily Value*
Total Fat 11.5g	**15%**
Saturated Fat 0.5g	**3%**
Cholesterol 0mg	**0%**
Sodium 0mg	**0%**
Total Carbohydrate 5g	**2%**
Dietary Fiber 0.1g	**0%**
Total Sugars 0.2g	
Protein 27.3g	
Calcium	0%
Iron	0%
Potassium 7mg	0%

The % Daily Value (DV) tells you how much a nutrient in a food serving contributes to a daily diet. 2,000 calorie a day is used for general nutrition advice.

Tadé Williams —
"I love it"

Recipe Serves

8 Servings

Ingredients	Amount	
Chicken breasts, with Skin & Bones	2	lb
Minced Garlic	2	tsp
Oregano, Dried	1	tsp
Pink Himalayan Salt— to taste		----
Lemon Juice	1	tbsp
Olive Oil / Coconut Oil (I used Olive)	2	tbsp
Black Pepper	1/4	tsp

Instructions

1. In a large cup or small bowl, add the following ingredients: oregano, olive oil, lemon juice, black pepper and minced garlic.
2. Stir until combined and set aside.
3. Cut the chicken into chunks. (I like to ask the butcher to do this part for me.)
4. Transfer the chicken to a large bowl.
5. Season the chicken with Salt to your taste.
6. Pour the wet seasoning mixture over the chicken and then get your hands into it! Make sure that each piece of chicken is coated with this FABULOUS seasoning.
7. Next, cover and allow to marinate for at least 30 minutes. If you marinate this overnight, the flavor will be even MORE AMAZING!
8. Transfer chicken to your air fryer. Be sure to leave enough space to turn each piece. Do not pack them in tight.
9. Cook at 400*F for 15 minutes.
10. Turn each piece of chicken and cook for another 13-15 minutes or until browned to your liking.

Notes

_____

_____

_____

_____

Air Fryer
Garlic Parmesan Wings

Lois Daniels --
"I'm not even on keto and this will be my Super Bowl wings! Thanks."

Someday's Here --
"These wings OMG! They are so good. Thank you."

Nutrition Facts

Servings: 8	
Amount per serving	
Calories	**599**
	% Daily Value*
Total Fat 44.4g	57%
Saturated Fat 15.2g	76%
Cholesterol 197mg	66%
Sodium 355mg	15%
Total Carbohydrate 1.7g	1%
Dietary Fiber 0.2g	1%
Total Sugars 0.1g	
Protein 44.6g	
Calcium	9%
Iron	13%
Potassium 382mg	8%

*The % Daily Value (DV) tells you how much a nutrient in a food serving contributes to a daily diet. 2,000 calorie a day is used for general nutrition advice.

Recipe Serves

6 Servings

Ingredients	Amount	
Wings (drumettes & wings)	3	lb
Salted, Butter	3	tbsp
Organic Rice Vinegar	1	tbsp
Mayo	1	tbsp
Minced Garlic	3	tbsp
Grated Parmesan Cheese	1/2	cup
Dried Parsley	1	tbsp
Black Pepper	1	tsp
Paprika (optional)	1/8	tsp
Cayenne Pepper (optional)	1/8	tsp
Salt to taste	----	

Instructions

1. In a microwavable bowl, melt the butter.
2. Add all ingredients to the bowl, mix well and set aside.
3. In a separate bowl or large baking dish season the wings to your taste with the salt.
4. Pour the wet seasoning over the wings and get messy! Massage the seasoning into the wings. Try to get it all over each wing and drumette.
5. Cover and allow them to marinate for at least 20-30 minutes. But if you let these marinate overnight...OMG! They will be even MORE AMAZING!
6. Transfer some wings to your air fryer.
7. Air Fry at 370*F for 6-13 minutes or until browned to your liking.
8. Turn them over and air fry for another 6-10 minutes or until browned to your liking.

No Air Fryer? — No Problem

1. Once the wings have marinated, transfer them to a baking dish.
2. Bake them in the oven at 375*F on the center rack for 35-45 minutes or until they are browned to your liking.
3. Turn them over and bake for another 10-15 minutes or until they are browned to your liking.

Notes
_____
_____
_____
_____

Air Fryer – Greek Chicken

"Enjoy this juicy chicken with my Marinated Summer Squash!"
—SoniaLee

Amudha Gopinathan --
"Superb making
in the air fryer."

saurabh negi --
"I used the recipe.
It was awesome.
Thanks!!!"

Nutrition Facts	
Servings: 4	
Amount per serving	
Calories	**339**
	% Daily Value*
Total Fat 21.2g	**27%**
Saturated Fat 4.2g	**21%**
Cholesterol 101mg	**34%**
Sodium 99mg	**4%**
Total Carbohydrate 3g	**1%**
Dietary Fiber 0.7g	**3%**
Total Sugars 0.1g	
Protein 33.4g	
Calcium	4%
Iron	13%
Potassium 327mg	7%

*The % Daily Value (DV) tells you how much a
nutrient in a food serving contributes to a daily diet.
2,000 calorie a day is used for general nutrition
advice.

Recipe Serves

4 Servings

Ingredients	Amount	
Chicken breasts: Boneless & Skinless	1	lb
Olive Oil	1/4	cup
Minced Garlic	2	tbsp
Organic red wine vinegar / Lemon Juice	2	tbsp
Dried oregano	1	tbsp
Thyme	1	tsp
Salt & Black Pepper to taste		----

Instructions

1. Cut the chicken breasts into cutlets.
2. Season the chicken cutlets with salt and black pepper to your taste and set aside.
3. In a small bowl or mug prepare the wet marinade. (minced garlic, thyme, dried oregano, red wine vinegar and olive oil).
4. Stir together until well blended.
5. Pour the wet marinade over the chicken cutlets. Make sure to coat each cutlet on all sides.
6. Allow to sit in marinade for 20-30 minutes.
7. Transfer chicken to your air fryer basket.
8. Cook for 10 minutes at 370*F.
9. Turn the cutlets over and cook for an additional 10 minutes.
10. Check temperature. Make sure it registers at 165*F.
11. You are now ready to enjoy this tender and juicy chicken!

Notes

_____

_____

_____

_____

Air Fryer – Pork Chops

"Enjoy these deliciously juicy chops with my Cucumber Avocado Salad!"
—SoniaLee

7smilesz--
"No way! Oh how I love pork chops!!! And the way you make them are delicious!!!"

glen sande--
"Just tried this tonight, and it was AWESOME! Very tender and juiccy chopes. I will definitely do this again!"

Nutrition Facts	
Servings: 4	
Amount per serving	
Calories	**348**
	% Daily Value*
Total Fat 20.3g	26%
Saturated Fat 6.3g	31%
Cholesterol 128mg	43%
Sodium 99mg	4%
Total Carbohydrate 1.3g	0%
Dietary Fiber 0.1g	0%
Total Sugars 0.2g	
Protein 37.2g	
Calcium	3%
Iron	7%
Potassium 25mg	1%

*The % Daily Value (DV) tells you how much a nutrient in a food serving contributes to a daily diet. 2,000 calorie a day is used for general nutrition advice.

Jenice Pye--
"Love, love, love your recipe."

Recipe Serves	
4-5 Servings	

Ingredients	Amount	
Center Cut Pork Chops	2	lb
Minced Garlic	2	tbsp
Lemon Juice	2	tbsp
Olive Oil (or Coconut Oil or Avocado Oil)	1 1/2	tbsp
Dried Parsley	1	tbsp
Pink Himalayan Salt to taste	----	
Black Pepper to taste	----	

Instructions

1. In a small bowl combine the minced garlic, lemon juice, olive oil and parsley. Mix until well-combined and set aside.
2. Season your pork chops with salt and pepper to your taste.
3. Pour the wet rub mixture over your chops and make sure to cover each chop, on all sides.
4. Allow to marinate at least 20 minutes. ***For the "WOW" factor, marinate over night!*
5. Transfer marinated pork chops to your air fryer.
6. Cook at 400*F for 8-10 minutes *or* until browned to your liking.
7. Then turn them over and cook for another 10-12 minutes *or* until browned to your liking.
8. Well done temperature is 170*F.

No Air Fryer? — No Problem

1. Bake *or* broil these chops.
2. Bake at 375*F for 40-50 minutes or until they are browned to your liking.
3. *Or* you can grill these bad boys!

Notes _____

_____

_____

_____

Chili with Black Soy Beans

"This is a recipe that our entire family loves! Enjoy!"
—SoniaLee

Nutrition Facts	
Servings: 5	
Amount per serving	
Calories	**419**
	% Daily Value*
Total Fat 14.9g	19%
Saturated Fat 4.8g	24%
Cholesterol 152mg	51%
Sodium 721mg	31%
Total Carbohydrate 10.5g	4%
Dietary Fiber 6.4g	23%
Total Sugars 2.1g	
Protein 60.1g	
Calcium	6%
Iron	192%
Potassium 1027mg	22%

*The % Daily Value (DV) tells you how much a nutrient in a food serving contributes to a daily diet. 2,000 calorie a day is used for general nutrition advice.

keto_restartann___
"Thanks to @ketowithlee I'll be making some #Keto #chili tonight for the family"

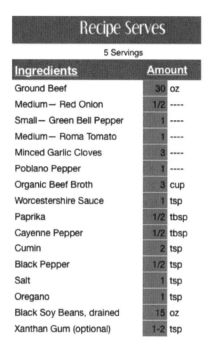

Recipe Serves		
5 Servings		
Ingredients	**Amount**	
Ground Beef	30	oz
Medium— Red Onion	1/2	----
Small— Green Bell Pepper	1	----
Medium— Roma Tomato	1	----
Minced Garlic Cloves	3	----
Poblano Pepper	1	----
Organic Beef Broth	3	cup
Worcestershire Sauce	1	tsp
Paprika	1/2	tbsp
Cayenne Pepper	1/2	tbsp
Cumin	2	tsp
Black Pepper	1/2	tsp
Salt	1	tsp
Oregano	1	tsp
Black Soy Beans, drained	15	oz
Xanthan Gum (optional)	1-2	tsp

Instructions

1. In a deep pot, brown the ground beef and do NOT drain. Ground turkey is also an option.
2. Add all of the spices and mix until well combined.
3. Add all of the veggies and do not forget the yummy garlic! Mix until well combined.
4. Add broth. Stir and bring to a boil.
5. Reduce the heat to a simmer, until it reaches the thickness you desire. You could add Xanthan Gum, 1 teaspoon at a time, until it is the thickness you want. This is an option, but not necessary.
6. Lastly, add the black soy beans and stir until combined.
7. Cook for another 5 minutes on low heat.
8. Serve this chili with avocado, sharp cheddar cheese, green onions, sour cream and low carb tortilla chips!!! AMAZING!

Notes

_____

_____

_____

_____

Chicken & Broccoli in Alfredo Sauce

"This is amazing over ZOODLES!"—SoniaLee

Nutrition Facts	
Servings: 8	
Amount per serving	
Calories	**306**
	% Daily Value*
Total Fat 26.1g	**34%**
Saturated Fat 15.8g	**79%**
Cholesterol 112mg	**41%**
Sodium 239mg	**10%**
Total Carbohydrate 3.9g	**1%**
Dietary Fiber 1g	**4%**
Total Sugars 1g	
Protein 15.5g	
Calcium	4%
Iron	6%
Potassium 124mg	3%

*The % Daily Value (DV) tells you how much a nutrient in a food serving contributes to a daily diet. 2,000 calorie a day is used for general nutrition advice.

Recipe Serves

8-10 Servings

Ingredients	Amount	
Chicken breasts, Boneless, Skinless Cubed	2	lb
Heavy Whipping Cream	2	cup
Minced Garlic	1	tbsp
Butter	1/2	cup
Parsley, dried	1/4	cup
Grated Parmesan Cheese	2	cup
Cream Cheese	2	oz
Red Bell Pepper / 1-7 oz can of Roasted Red Peppers	1	----
Broccoli Florets	2	cup
Oregano, Dried	1	tsp
Salt & Black Pepper to taste		----
Organic Chicken Broth	2	cup

Instructions

1. In a deep pot over medium heat, melt the butter.
2. Add garlic and cook until fragrant.
3. Add the chicken and season with salt and black pepper to your taste.
4. Once the chicken is browned, add the heavy whipping cream, cream cheese, parsley, oregano and chicken broth. (Start with one cup of chicken broth). Stir until well combined and bring to a boil.
5. ****TIP****I use the broth to help make more sauce and to thin the sauce, if needed.
6. Once it is boiling, reduce heat to a simmer and add parmesan cheese. Let simmer until the sauce has thickened to your liking.
7. Lastly, add the broccoli and red bell pepper. Stir until combined.
8. Continue to simmer until the broccoli is fork tender.
9. Allow to cool for at least 5 minutes before serving.
10. Now it is ready to serve!

Notes

_____

_____

_____

_____

Chicken Parmesan

"This goes lovely over zoodles or paired with my tasty arugula salad."
—SoniaLee

Gena Brown —
"This recipe was amazing! It was a hit in my house and I will be making it again soon! Thanks ketowithlee!"

thehennagoddess —
"Crispy and stringy chicken parmesan. Immense and enough for 2 days"

Ashley H—
"Made this tonight and it was a hit! I paired it with garlic parm zoodles! Thanks"

Thalia Sanchez—
"This was sooooo goood!! I used Rao's marinara sauce and it worked perfect! I fried my chicken in avocado oil in a non stick skillet and it worked for me. Thank you for this delish recipe!"

Nutrition Facts

Amount per serving	
Calories	**313**
	% Daily Value*
Total Fat 12g	15%
Saturated Fat 6.4g	32%
Cholesterol 152mg	51%
Sodium 863mg	38%
Total Carbohydrate 5.4g	2%
Dietary Fiber 1.3g	5%
Total Sugars 2.5g	
Protein 48.7g	
Calcium	21%
Iron	8%
Potassium 583mg	12%

*The % Daily Value (DV) tells you how much a nutrient in a food serving contributes to a daily diet. 2,000 calorie a day is used for general nutrition advice.

Notes _____

_____

_____

_____

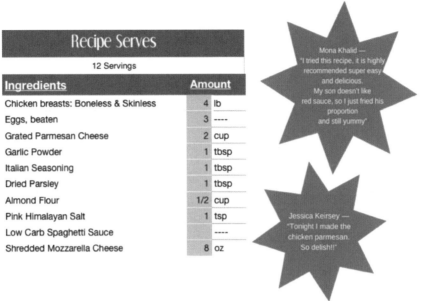

Recipe Serves		
12 Servings		
Ingredients	**Amount**	
Chicken breasts: Boneless & Skinless	4	lb
Eggs, beaten	3	----
Grated Parmesan Cheese	2	cup
Garlic Powder	1	tbsp
Italian Seasoning	1	tbsp
Dried Parsley	1	tbsp
Almond Flour	1/2	cup
Pink Himalayan Salt	1	tsp
Low Carb Spaghetti Sauce	----	
Shredded Mozzarella Cheese	8	oz

Mona Khalid —
"I tried this recipe, it is highly recommended super easy and delicious.
My son doesn't like red sauce, so I just fried his proportion and still yummy"

Jessica Keirsey —
"Tonight I made the chicken parmesan.
So delish!!"

Instructions

1. Cut the chicken breasts into cutlets and set aside.
2. Season the chicken cutlets with salt and black pepper to your taste and set them aside.
3. Beat the eggs and pour them into a small bowl or shallow dish and set it aside.
4. In a separate small bowl or shallow dish prepare the breading. Combine the parmesan cheese, garlic powder, salt, parsley, almond flour and the Italian seasoning. Mix well and set aside.
5. Now it's time to give the chicken an egg bath!
6. Dip the chicken into the eggs and then immediately into the breading mixture. Be sure to coat all sides. ****This is a light breading mixture. If you would like the breading thicker, return the chicken to the egg wash and then the breading mixture again. It's that simple.*
7. The next step is to fry the chicken until it is browned on both sides. Typically, this takes approximately 3-5 minutes on each side. ****I fry these in either coconut or olive oil on medium-high heat.*
8. While the chicken is frying, pour your spaghetti sauce into a large and deep baking dish.
9. Once the chicken is cooked, transfer it to the baking dish and sprinkle shredded mozzarella over the top of each piece.
10. Now off to the oven to bake at 350*F for 20-30 minutes or until golden brown to your liking.
11. Allow to cool for at least 5-10 minutes before serving. Enjoy!

Chicken Tenders

"I put a wooden spoon in the center of the pan. When the spoon begins to sizzle, the oil is hot and ready for the chicken."
—SoniaLee

Nutrition Facts	
Servings: 6	
Amount per serving	
Calories	**387**
	% Daily Value*
Total Fat 17.8g	**23%**
Saturated Fat 6.2g	**31%**
Cholesterol 177mg	**59%**
Sodium 329mg	**14%**
Total Carbohydrate 1.3g	**0%**
Dietary Fiber 0.4g	**1%**
Total Sugars 0.5g	
Protein 50.6g	
Calcium	15%
Iron	12%
Potassium 386mg	8%

*The % Daily Value (DV) tells you how much a nutrient in a food serving contributes to a daily diet. 2,000 calorie a day is used for general nutrition advice.

Recipe Serves

6 Servings

Ingredient	Amount	
Chicken Breasts: Boneless & Skinless	2	lb
Almond Flour	1/2	cup
Grated Parmesan Cheese	1 1/2	cup
Italian Seasoning	3	tsp
Garlic Powder	1	tsp
Black Pepper	1/2	tsp
Egg, beaten (use more if needed)	1	----

Instructions

1. Cut the chicken breasts into strips and transfer them to a large bowl.
2. In a small bowl scramble, the egg and pour it into a shallow dish.
3. In a separate bowl combine the almond flour, grated parmesan cheese, Italian seasoning, garlic powder and black pepper. Stir until well combined.
4. On medium-high heat, heat up your oil while you bread the chicken strips. I use olive oil, but you can use avocado or coconut oil. Some people like to use bacon grease or lard.
5. Now for the assembly line. Dip the chicken strips into the egg and then into the breading and transfer them to a baking dish.
6. Repeat this step until all chicken strips are coated. Now you are ready to begin frying.
7. Fry the chicken until golden brown to your liking or until the temperature reaches 165*F.

Notes

_____

_____

_____

_____

Eggplant Lasagna

"This is a great dish to use for meal prepping. This meal freezes great if you want to make it ahead for dinner during your busy work week."
—SoniaLee

Remi Martin —
"I had your eggplant
dish and it was
AMAZING!!!!!!!"

Recipe Serves

8 Servings

Ingredients	Amount	
Medium Eggplant	1	----
Garlic Cloves, minced	6	----
Small Red Onion	90	g
Ground Beef	1	lb
Shredded Mozzarella	140	g
Whole Milk Ricotta	82	g
Shredded Parmesan Cheese	84	g
Crushed Tomatoes / Tomato Pureé	28	oz
Classico Spinach & Cheese Florentine Spaghetti Sauce (or your favorite low carb sauce)	24	oz
Fresh Baby Spinach	128	g
Olive Oil (or your choice of oil: coconut or avocado)	1	tbsp
Seasoning of your choice to taste: Italian seasoning or dried oregano		----

Nutrition Facts

Servings: 8

Amount per serving

Calories	202
	% Daily Value*
Total Fat 12g	**15%**
Saturated Fat 4.3g	**21%**
Cholesterol 52mg	**17%**
Sodium 167mg	**7%**
Total Carbohydrate 7.2g	**3%**
Dietary Fiber 2.7g	**10%**
Total Sugars 3g	
Protein 16.6g	
Calcium	4%
Iron	12%
Potassium 482mg	10%

*The % Daily Value (DV) tells you how much a nutrient in a food serving contributes to a daily diet. 2,000 calorie a day is used for general nutrition advice.

Instructions

1. Pre-heat your oven to 350*F.
2. Peel the eggplant and slice it into circles. These slices need to be approximately ¼" thick. (You can slice it lengthwise as well - up to you).
3. Lay the slices out on a baking sheet and salt them. Allow them to sweat for at least 30 minutes. This step will prevent the lasagna from being watery!
4. After 30 minutes, pat them dry and spray them with oil.
5. Bake them for 25 minutes at 350*F or until golden brown and set them aside.
6. While the eggplant is baking – Pour olive oil into a pan and sauté the garlic and onions until fragrant.
7. Add the ground beef, spinach and all seasoning.
8. Once the meat is browned and the spinach, crushed tomatoes and spaghetti sauce. Stir until combined.
9. Let simmer until the sauce thickens to your liking. It usually takes approximately 20 minutes.
10. Now that the eggplant and meat is done, we are ready for the fun part!
11. Layer your dish as follows:
    a. Meat sauce, eggplant, meat sauce, cheeses, eggplant, meat sauce, cheeses. Repeat until you get to the top of your baking dish and top it with cheese.
12. Bake at 350*F for 25 minutes or until the top is golden brown.
13. Allow this dish to cool for at least 5-10 minutes before serving.
14. Also, allow this dish to cool completely before transferring it to an airtight container.

Notes _____

_____

_____

_____

Fried Fish
with Homemade Tartar Sauce

FISH | TARTAR SAUCE

Nutrition Facts	
Servings: 8	
Amount per serving	
Calories	**492**
	% Daily Value*
Total Fat 33.5g	**43%**
Saturated Fat 8.8g	**44%**
Cholesterol 105mg	**35%**
Sodium 1143mg	**50%**
Total Carbohydrate 0.9g	**0%**
Dietary Fiber 0.4g	**1%**
Total Sugars 0.3g	
Protein 35.6g	
Calcium	23%
Iron	4%
Potassium 599mg	13%

*The % Daily Value (DV) tells you how much a nutrient in a food serving contributes to a daily diet. 2,000 calorie a day is used for general nutrition advice.

Nutrition Facts	
Servings: 16 (1 TBSP EACH)	
Amount per serving	
Calories	**121**
	% Daily Value*
Total Fat 12g	**15%**
Saturated Fat 2g	**10%**
Cholesterol 10mg	**3%**
Sodium 272mg	**12%**
Total Carbohydrate 2.1g	**1%**
Dietary Fiber 0g	**0%**
Total Sugars 0.1g	
Protein 0g	
Calcium	0%
Iron	0%
Potassium 2mg	0%

*The % Daily Value (DV) tells you how much a nutrient in a food serving contributes to a daily diet. 2,000 calorie a day is used for general nutrition advice.

Recipe Serves - Cod Fish

8 Servings

Ingredients	Amount	
Cod Fish (fresh or frozen)	2	lb
Almond Flour (or coconut flour)	1/4	cup
Grated Parmesan Cheese	1 1/2	cup
Italian Seasoning	3	tsp
Garlic Powder	2	tsp
Black Pepper	1/2	tsp
Dried Parsley	3	tsp
Eggs, beaten	----	

Tartar Sauce

16 Servings (1 Tablespoon Each)

Ingredients	Amount	
Mayo (low carb)	2	cup
Dill Relish	1/2	cup
Yellow Mustard	1	tsp
Cayenne Pepper (optional)	1/2	tsp

Instructions – Cod Fish

1. In a small bowl, beat the eggs and out them aside.
2. In a shallow dish combine the parmesan cheese, almond flour, parsley, Italian seasoning, garlic powder and black pepper. Mix well and set aside.
3. Now for the assembly line and heat oil on medium-high heat.
4. Dip the fish into the egg and then into the breading and transfer to a plate until oil is ready.
5. Repeat these steps until all the fish pieces are coated.
6. Now you are ready to fry these bad boys!

Instructions – Tartar Sauce

1. In a small bowl combine the mayo, dill relish, yellow mustard and cayenne pepper.
2. Mix well, cover and refrigerate until ready to use.

Notes _____

_____

_____

_____

Parmesan Crusted Eggplant

"This coupled with my meat sauce is divine!"
—SoniaLee

Nutrition Facts	
Servings: 7	
Amount per serving	
Calories	**150**
	% Daily Value*
Total Fat 9.5g	12%
Saturated Fat 5.4g	27%
Cholesterol 28mg	9%
Sodium 669mg	29%
Total Carbohydrate 5.5g	2%
Dietary Fiber 1.9g	7%
Total Sugars 1.9g	
Protein 12.9g	
Calcium	26%
Iron	1%
Potassium 119mg	3%

*The % Daily Value (DV) tells you how much a nutrient in a food serving contributes to a daily diet. 2,000 calorie a day is used for general nutrition advice.

Taylor Hunter —
"I'm excited about this recipe, I've been looking for a good keto eggplant recipe. Thank you for making such amazing videos!!"

christianasconscience —
"This is really original"

Notes

_____

_____

_____

_____

Recipe Serves

7 Servings (depends on how thick you slice them.)

Ingredients	Amount	
Eggplant (medium or half of a large one)	1	----
Eggs, beaten for wash	2	----
Non-Stick Spray (Coconut, Olive Oil or Avocado Oil)		----
Grated Parmesan Cheese	2	cup
Garlic Powder	1	tbsp
Italian Seasoning	1	tbsp
Parsley	1	tbsp
Almond Flour	1/2	cup
Pink Himalayan Salt	1	tsp

Instructions

1. Pre-heat your oven to 400*F.
2. Wash the eggplant and pat it dry.
3. Next, cut the eggplant into slices and transfer them to a baking sheet. You can cut them into circles or lengthwise.
4. Sprinkle salt onto the eggplant and pace them aside to sweat for 20-30 minutes.
5. While the eggplant is sweating, prepare your breading and your egg bath.
6. In a small bowl combine the almond flour, salt, parsley, Italian seasoning, grated parmesan cheese, and garlic powder. Mix well and set aside.
7. In a separate bowl, beat the eggs and set aside.
8. Pat the sweat off with a clean paper towel.
9. Dip the sliced eggplant into the egg wash and then into the breading and place them on a baking sheet.
10. Freeze them for 10-15 minutes, no less.
11. Spray the eggplant with non-stick spray.
12. Broil these on high for 7 minutes or until golden brown and then turn them over and broil for another 7 minutes or until golden brown.

Pork Tenderloin

 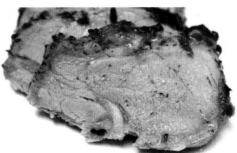

Doris Feliciano —
"DELISH!!!!"

Nutrition Facts	
Servings: 8	
Amount per serving	
Calories	**212**
	% Daily Value*
Total Fat 9.3g	**12%**
Saturated Fat 2.1g	**11%**
Cholesterol 83mg	**28%**
Sodium 920mg	**40%**
Total Carbohydrate 1.1g	**0%**
Dietary Fiber 0.3g	**1%**
Total Sugars 0g	
Protein 29.9g	
Calcium	1%
Iron	9%
Potassium 497mg	11%

*The % Daily Value (DV) tells you how much
a nutrient in a food serving contributes to a
daily diet.2,000 calorie a day is used for
general nutrition advice.

Recipe Serves

8 Servings

Ingredients	Amount	
Pork Tenderloin	2	lb
Lemon Juice	5	tbsp
Minced Garlic	2	tbsp
Pink Himalayan Salt	3	tsp
Black pepper	1	tsp
Olive Oil	3	tbsp
Oregano	2	tsp

Instructions

1. Pre-heat your oven to 375*F.
2. Make sure that your pork tenderloin is brought to room temperature. Transfer your tenderloin to a deep baking dish.
3. In a small bowl combine the following: lemon juice, minced garlic, salt, black pepper, olive oil and oregano. Stir until well combined. *** You can use avocado or coconut oil instead. Remember to adjust your macros accordingly.
4. Pour the mixture over the pork tenderloin. Try to cover all sides.
5. Allow to sit and marinate for 20-30 minutes. Overnight is soooo much better!
6. Drain the excess juices. The tenderloin will release its own juices.
7. Bake at 375*F or 35-45 minutes. Baste the meat with its juices.
8. Check the temperature to ensure it is cooked thoroughly. Perfect temperature for pork is 170*F. *** Every oven is different. I had to return my tenderloin to bake for another 20 minutes to get it to temperature.
9. Now, broil on high for 5 minutes or until golden brown.

Notes
_____

_____

_____

_____

Roasted Cod

Recipe Serves

8 Servings

Ingredients	Amount	
Cod (fresh or frozen), unsalted and skinless	2	lb
Red Bell Peppers (medium)	2	----
Orange Bell Pepper (medium)	1	----
Yellow Bell Pepper (medium)	1	----
Red Onion (small)	1	----
Olive Oil	6	tbsp
Pink Himalayan Salt to taste		----
Black pepper to taste		----
Garlic Cloves (minced)	8	----
Organic Red Wine Vinegar	4	tbsp
Fresh Parsley, stems removed and roughly chopped	1/4	cup
Drained Capers	2	tbsp
Dried Oregano	1	tsp
Cayenne Pepper (optional)	1/2	tsp

Nutrition Facts

Servings: 8

Amount per serving

Calories	204
	% Daily Value*
Total Fat 11.6g	15%
Saturated Fat 1.5g	8%
Cholesterol 41mg	14%
Sodium 169mg	7%
Total Carbohydrate 5.2g	2%
Dietary Fiber 1.5g	5%
Total Sugars 2.5g	
Protein 21.2g	
Calcium	2%
Iron	4%
Potassium 41mg	1%

*The % Daily Value (DV) tells you how much a nutrient in a food serving contributes to a daily diet. 2,000 calorie a day is used for general nutrition advice.

Instructions – Roasted Red Peppers

1. Move the oven rack to the top most position then turn broiler on high.
2. Seed and cut the bell peppers into halves, lengthwise.
3. Lay the peppers onto a lined baking sheet. *I use parchment paper. It is easy to use and allows for a quick clean up!*
4. Drizzle olive oil over the peppers and then sprinkle them with salt and black pepper to your taste. *You can use avocado oil or coconut oil instead.*
5. Toss to coat the peppers and place skin side down onto the sheet.
6. Broil for 10 minutes or until blackened and turn them over.
7. Broil for another 10 minutes or until blackened.
8. Transfer the peppers with all the juices to a bowl and cover with plastic wrap.
9. Let it sit for 20 minutes to steam and cool.
10. Meanwhile, move the oven rack to the center of the oven and pre-heat oven to 300*F.

Instructions - Assembly

1. Check the peppers. If they are cool to the touch, begin to peel the skin off of them and tear them into strips. Then transfer them to a large bowl.
2. Add the following to the bowl: onions, garlic, vinegar, oregano, cayenne, parsley and capers. Mix well and set aside.
3. Place your cod into your baking dish.
4. Pour your seasoning and vegetables over your cod. Sprinkle with salt and black pepper to your taste.
5. Roast until the flesh is opaque throughout and flakes easily with a fork when pressed. This takes approximately 25 to 35 minutes. *Check at 25 minutes. Each oven is different.*
6. Allow to cool for 10 minutes before serving.

Notes _____

_____

_____

_____

Shrimp Scampi

"This goes great over cauliflower rice or zoodles!"
—SoniaLee

flakitabella30 —
"Yum"

Gena Brown --
"I did this and added
broccoli. OMG! It was
a good meal."

Nutrition Facts	
Servings: 6	
Amount per serving	
Calories	**600**
	% Daily Value*
Total Fat 54.4g	**70%**
Saturated Fat 17.2g	**86%**
Cholesterol 207mg	**75%**
Sodium 902mg	**39%**
Total Carbohydrate 5.4g	**2%**
Dietary Fiber 0.7g	**2%**
Total Sugars 4.7g	
Protein 25g	
Calcium	18%
Iron	12%
Potassium 98mg	2%

*The % Daily Value (DV) tells you how much a nutrient in a food serving contributes to a daily diet. 2,000 calorie a day is used for general nutrition advice.

Recipe Serves

6 Servings

Ingredients	Amount	
Extra Large Peeled & Deveined Shrimp	1	lb
Juiced Lemons	6	----
Chopped Red Onion (medium)	1/2	----
Grated Parmesan Cheese	1/4	cup
Olive Oil (or coconut / avocado oil)	1/4	cup
Minced Garlic	2	tbsp
Butter Stick, un-salted	1	----
Dried Parsley	1/4	cup
Dried Oregano	1/2	tbsp
Pink Himalayan Salt	1	tsp
Black Pepper	1/2	tsp

Instructions

1. In a pan, over medium heat, sauté onions and garlic in butter until onions are translucent.
2. Add olive oil, herbs and lemon juice. Stir until combined. *** *You can use coconut or avocado oil instead. Remember to adjust the macros accordingly.*
3. Now you can add the salt, black pepper, cheese and shrimp. Stir until well combined.
4. Reduce the heat to low-heat.
5. Simmer until the shrimp are a vibrant pink. Approximately, 5 -6 minutes, MAX. If you see the tails starting to curl, remove the pan from the burner. They are done!

Notes

_____

_____

_____

_____

<u>SIDE DISH</u>

Arugula Salad
With Homemade Vinaigrette

"This is super easy to make, and it packs a lot of flavor. Great for busy people."
—SoniaLee

Nutrition Facts	
Servings: 2	
Amount per serving	
Calories	**69**
	% Daily Value*
Total Fat 7.1g	9%
Saturated Fat 1g	5%
Cholesterol 0mg	0%
Sodium 46mg	2%
Total Carbohydrate 2.1g	1%
Dietary Fiber 0.3g	1%
Total Sugars 0.4g	
Protein 0.7g	
Calcium	3%
Iron	2%
Potassium 91mg	2%

*The % Daily Value (DV) tells you how much a nutrient in a food serving contributes to a daily diet. 2,000 calorie a day is used for general nutrition advice.

Recipe Serves

2 Servings

Ingredients	Amount	
Arugula	2	cup
Shallot, chopped	1	----
Olive Oil (or your favorite oil: Coconut/ Avocado)	1	tbsp
Organic Apple Cider Vinegar	2	tbsp
Brown Spicy Mustard	1	tsp

Instructions

1. In a large bowl, combine the shallot, olive oil, apple cider vinegar and the brown spicy mustard. Stir until well combined. *** *You can use coconut oil (the liquid form oil) or avocado oil instead. Remember to adjust the macros accordingly.*
2. Add the arugula and toss until it is well covered. You could also put this in a zip lock bag and shaky shaky shaky.

Notes

_____

_____

_____

_____

Asparagus with Bacon

"Super easy and such bold flavor!"
—SoniaLee

7smilesz —
"Yummm! With bacon!!! O man makes it ten times better."

Nutrition Facts	
Servings: 4	
Amount per serving	
Calories	**107**
	% Daily Value*
Total Fat 7.5g	10%
Saturated Fat 4.3g	22%
Cholesterol 10mg	3%
Sodium 222mg	10%
Total Carbohydrate 5.2g	2%
Dietary Fiber 2.4g	9%
Total Sugars 2.2g	
Protein 6.1g	
Calcium	2%
Iron	15%
Potassium 291mg	6%

*The % Daily Value (DV) tells you how much a nutrient in a food serving contributes to a daily diet. 2,000 calorie a day is used for general nutrition advice.

Recipe Serves

4 Servings

Ingredients	Amount	
Asparagus	1	lb
Coconut Oil (or Olive/Avocado Oil)	1	tbsp
Minced Garlic	1	tbsp
Bacon Strips	2	----
Pink Himalayan Salt to taste		----
Black Pepper to taste		----

Instructions

1. Cook the bacon. I prefer to bake my bacon in the oven at 425*F for 15-20 minutes. Set it aside to cool and then roughly chop it up. Keep it handy, you will need it in a few minutes.
2. In a pan, over medium heat, add oil and sauté the minced garlic until it is browned, NOT BURNT!
3. Transfer the bacon to the pan and add the asparagus.
4. Season with salt and black pepper to your taste. Toss until well combined.
5. Now, cook until the asparagus is fork tender.

Notes

_____

_____

_____

_____

Brussels & Bacon

"Don't feel like making this on the stove top? Put it all together and bake it!"
—SoniaLee

Nutrition Facts	
Servings: 6	
Amount per serving	
Calories	**49**
	% Daily Value*
Total Fat 1.5g	2%
Saturated Fat 0.5g	3%
Cholesterol 3mg	1%
Sodium 43mg	2%
Total Carbohydrate 7.7g	3%
Dietary Fiber 2.8g	10%
Total Sugars 2g	
Protein 3.2g	
Calcium	3%
Iron	5%
Potassium 359mg	8%

*The % Daily Value (DV) tells you how much a nutrient in a food serving contributes to a daily diet. 2,000 calorie a day is used for general nutrition advice.

Serrano Ricardo —
"OMG!!!!! this was so so good cant wait to try another dish from keto lee... thanks"

Doris Feliciano —
"I loved this dish so much, I did not want to share."

7smilesz —
"This is so mouth watering lol*r."

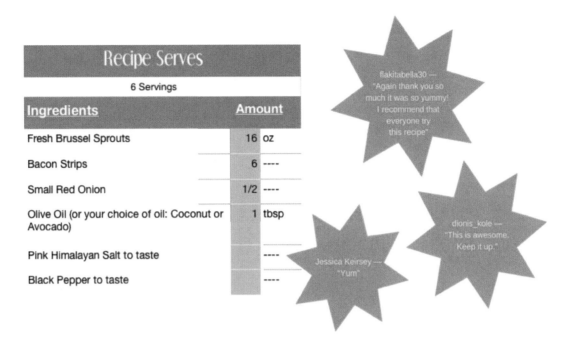

Recipe Serves		
6 Servings		
Ingredients	**Amount**	
Fresh Brussel Sprouts	16	oz
Bacon Strips	6	----
Small Red Onion	1/2	----
Olive Oil (or your choice of oil: Coconut or Avocado)	1	tbsp
Pink Himalayan Salt to taste		----
Black Pepper to taste		----

flakitabella30 — "Again thank you so much it was so yummy! I recommend that everyone try this recipe"

dionis_kole — "This is awesome. Keep it up."

Jessica Keirsey — "Yum"

Instructions

1. Bake the bacon in the oven at 425*F for 15-20 minutes, or until baked to your liking.
2. Spray a large pan with non-stick spray. I like to use the coconut oil spray, but you can use the olive oil, avocado oil or bacon grease.
3. Allow the bacon to cool and then chop it up, transfer it to the greased pan and set it aside.
4. Chop up the red onion and add it to the bacon.
5. Shred or chop the Brussel sprouts and add these to the pan.
6. Season with salt and black pepper to your taste. Stir until well combined.
7. Cook over medium heat until the Brussel sprouts are tender, Not mushy!
8. Remove from heat and serve.

Notes _____

_____

_____

_____

Chessy Broccoli
with Cheddar Cheese Sauce

\

Recipe Serves

18 Servings

Ingredients	Amount	
Broccoli Florets	3	lb
Heavy Whipping Cream	3 1/2	cup
Garlic powder	2	tsp
Butter	5	tbsp
Parsley, dried	1	tbsp
Grated Parmesan Cheese	2	cup
Pink Himalayan Salt	1	tsp
Cayenne Pepper	1/4	tsp
White Pepper / Black Pepper	1/4	tsp
Extra Sharp Cheddar Cheese	5	cup

barbarasuemiller —
"Yum!"

Nutrition Facts

Servings: 18	
Amount per serving	
Calories	**290**
	% Daily Value*
Total Fat 24.2g	31%
Saturated Fat 14g	70%
Cholesterol 75mg	25%
Sodium 461mg	20%
Total Carbohydrate 7.1g	3%
Dietary Fiber 2.3g	8%
Total Sugars 1.4g	
Protein 14g	
Calcium	29%
Iron	3%
Potassium 263mg	6%

*The % Daily Value (DV) tells you how much a nutrient in a food serving contributes to a daily diet. 2,000 calorie a day is used for general nutrition advice.

Instructions – Broccoli

1. Pre-heat your oven to 400*F.
2. In a large pot bring the chicken broth or water to a boil.
3. Add the broccoli and cook until fork tender.
4. Drain and set aside.

Instructions – Topping

1. In a small microwavable bowl, melt 1 tablespoon of butter.
2. Add 1 cup of parmesan cheese, 1 cup of cheddar cheese, parsley and garlic powder.
3. Mix until well combined and set aside.

Instructions – Cheddar Cheese Sauce

1. In a large pot add the following: heavy whipping cream, cheeses and spices. Stir until well combined and cook over medium heat.
2. Stir frequently to avoid burning or scorching.
3. Once the cheeses have melted and are smooth, remove the pot from the burner and set it aside.

Instructions – Assembly

1. Transfer the broccoli to a deep baking dish.
2. Pour the cheese sauce over the broccoli and mix until all of the broccoli is covered.
3. Sprinkle the topping over the top of the broccoli and press it down as flat as possible.
4. Bake at 400*F for 25-35 minutes or until the top is golden brown and bubbling.
5. Allow to cool at least 5-10 minutes to avoid burning the roof of your mouth.

Notes _____

_____

_____

_____

Cucumber Avocado Salad

"Serve this with my Pork Chops!"
—SoniaLee

7smilesz —
"One of my favorites!
So yummy!"

Barberscientist —
"That was delicious"

Nutrition Facts	
Servings: 6	
Amount per serving	
Calories	**85**
	% Daily Value*
Total Fat 6.6g	8%
Saturated Fat 2.1g	10%
Cholesterol 8mg	3%
Sodium 110mg	5%
Total Carbohydrate 5.8g	2%
Dietary Fiber 2.6g	9%
Total Sugars 1.8g	
Protein 2.4g	
Calcium	5%
Iron	3%
Potassium 261mg	6%

*The % Daily Value (DV) tells you how much a nutrient in a food serving contributes to a daily diet. 2,000 calorie a day is used for general nutrition advice.

Recipe Serves

6 Servings

Ingredients	Amount	
English Cucumber (seedless), Chopped	1	----
Shallot, chopped	1	----
Grape tomatoes, cut into halves	2	oz
Avocado, chopped	1	----
Dried Oregano	1	tsp
Feta Cheese Crumbles	2	oz
Olive Oil	1	tbsp
Fresh Lime Juice	2	tbsp

Instructions

1. In a large bowl combine all of the vegetables.
2. Add all of the seasonings and stir until well combined.
3. Keep this salad refrigerated in an airtight container for up to 1 week!

Notes _____

_____

_____

_____

Jalapeño Chips

"These are fantastic with bun-less burgers!"
—SoniaLee

"If you are allergic to the almond flour you can opt to use coconut flour or more parmesan cheese instead. Just remember to adjust the macros accordingly."
—SoniaLee

Nutrition Facts	
Servings: 6	
Amount per serving	
Calories	**64**
	% Daily Value*
Total Fat 3.9g	5%
Saturated Fat 1.1g	5%
Cholesterol 4mg	1%
Sodium 64mg	3%
Total Carbohydrate 3.7g	1%
Dietary Fiber 1g	3%
Total Sugars 1.7g	
Protein 2.4g	
Calcium	6%
Iron	3%
Potassium 102mg	2%

*The % Daily Value (DV) tells you how much a nutrient in a food serving contributes to a daily diet. 2,000 calorie a day is used for general nutrition advice.

howudish --
"Love it!...,"

Recipe Serves		
6 Servings		
Ingredients	**Amount**	
Grated Parmesan Cheese	2	cup
Garlic Powder	1	tbsp
Italian Seasoning	1	tbsp
Parsley	1	tbsp
Almond Flour	1/2	cup
Pink Himalayan Salt	1	tsp
Jalapeños	4	----
Eggs, beaten	2	----
Olive Oil (or Coconut or Avocado Oil)		----

Instructions

1. In a small bowl combine the following: parmesan, garlic powder, Italian seasoning, parsley, almond flour and salt. Mix until well combined and set aside. ****This breading can be prepared ahead of time. Keep it refrigerated in an airtight container until ready to use.*
2. Wash the jalapeños and pat them dry.
3. Cut off both ends of the jalapeños.
4. Slice the jalapeños and dunk them into the egg bath and then into the breading.
5. Now, transfer them to a freezer friendly plate or bowl. Freeze for 10-15 minutes.
6. In a pan, heat the oil over medium heat. You can use either coconut, avocado or olive oil.
7. Once the oil is hot, place the slices one at a time into the pan. Fry them until lightly browned and then turn them.
8. Fry until lightly browned, to your liking.

Notes _____

_____

_____

_____

Marinated Summer Squash

"This is a great addition to any main dish!"
—SoniaLee

Vickie Cook —
"Looks yummy!!
Another great
vegetable recipe!!"

Nutrition Facts	
Servings: 4	
Amount per serving	
Calories	**85**
	% Daily Value*
Total Fat 7.3g	9%
Saturated Fat 1.1g	5%
Cholesterol 0mg	0%
Sodium 887mg	39%
Total Carbohydrate 5.3g	2%
Dietary Fiber 1.7g	6%
Total Sugars 2.6g	
Protein 1.8g	
Calcium	2%
Iron	3%
Potassium 392mg	8%

*The % Daily Value (DV) tells you how much a nutrient in a food serving contributes to a daily diet. 2,000 calorie a day is used for general nutrition advice.

Recipe Serves

4 Servings

Ingredients	Amount	
Medium Summer Squash	3	----
Salt — to make squash sweat	1 1/2	tsp
Olive / Coconut Oil	2	tbsp
Minced Garlic	1	tsp
Rice Vinegar	2	tbsp
Swerve (or—your favorite sugar substitute)	1/2	tsp
Cayenne Pepper	1/4	tsp
Black Pepper	1/4	tsp

Instructions

1. Cut the squash into chunks or circles and place them in a large bowl.
2. Season with salt and set aside to sweat for 10 minutes.
3. Meanwhile, in a large bowl mix together the following: garlic, vinegar, sugar substitute, cayenne pepper, black pepper and 2 tablespoons oil. You can use coconut, avocado or olive oil. Be sure to adjust the macros accordingly.
4. Stir until well combined.
5. Remove moisture from the squash by patting it dry with a paper towel.
6. Pour mixture over the squash and stir until all pieces are coated.
7. Transfer squash to a pan and cook over medium-high heat until golden brown. This takes approximately 5 minutes. *** *You could also make this in the oven. Bake it at 375*F for 14-16 minutes*
8. Now reduce the heat to medium-low heat and cover.
9. Cook until for tender, approximately 15 minutes.

Notes

_____

_____

_____

"Potato Salad" Two Styles
With the Daikon Radish

"Oh my! Oh my! This is superb with my Roast Pork or Pavo-Chon!"
—SoniaLee

lantina_n_keto —
"So i love potato salad but
obviously thats not keto.
@keto_with_lee has an
amazing recipe for faux potato
salad....im so glad im having
some tonight with my peril."

Recipe Serves

4 Servings

Ingredients -Daikon Puerto Rican Style	Amount	
Daikon, cut into cubes	1	lb
Mayo (low carb)	4	tbsp
Green Bell Pepper, chopped	1/4	cup
Small Red Onion, Chopped	1/4	cup
Eggs, Hard boiled & Chopped	2	----
Olives, chopped	2	tbsp
Pink Himalayan Salt to taste		----
Black Pepper to taste		----

Nutrition Facts - Daikon

Servings: 4

Amount per serving

Calories	117

	% Daily Value*
Total Fat 7.5g	10%
Saturated Fat 0.7g	3%
Cholesterol 87mg	29%
Sodium 298mg	13%
Total Carbohydrate 7.9g	3%
Dietary Fiber 2.6g	9%
Total Sugars 4g	
Protein 5.2g	
Calcium	1%
Iron	3%
Potassium 307mg	7%

*The % Daily Value (DV) tells you how much a nutrient in a food serving contributes to a daily diet. 2,000 calorie a day is used for general nutrition advice.

Instructions – Puerto Rican Style

1. Peel the Daikon and cut it into cubes.
2. Boil them in salted water until they are fork tender. Not Mushy! Then drain them and set them aside to cool for 5 minutes.
3. Transfer the daikon to a large bowl and add the following: green peppers, onions, olives, mayo and eggs. Stir until well combined.
4. Season with salt and black pepper to your taste. You can add some cayenne pepper for spice if you'd like. Stir again until combined.
5. Keep in an airtight container for up to 3-4 days. After 3-4 days the radishes turn sour.

Notes

_____

_____

_____

_____

Recipe Serves

4 Servings

Ingredients -Daikon With A Twist	Amount	
Daikon, cut into cubes	1	lb
Mayo (low carb)	4	tbsp
Bacon Strips, coarsely chopped	2	----
Gorgonzola Crumbles	2	tbsp
Green Onions, chopped	1	tbsp
Pink Himalayan Salt to taste		----
Black Pepper to taste		----

Nutrition Facts - Daikon

Servings: 4

Amount per serving

Calories	134

	% Daily Value*
Total Fat 9.2g	12%
Saturated Fat 2.1g	11%
Cholesterol 19mg	6%
Sodium 396mg	17%
Total Carbohydrate 6.9g	3%
Dietary Fiber 2.3g	8%
Total Sugars 3.3g	
Protein 6.7g	
Calcium	2%
Iron	1%
Potassium 329mg	7%

*The % Daily Value (DV) tells you how much a nutrient in a food serving contributes to a daily diet. 2,000 calorie a day is used for general nutrition advice.

Instructions – A Twist

1. Peel the Daikon and cut it into cubes.
2. Boil them in salted water until they are fork tender. Not Mushy! Then drain them and set them aside to cool for 5 minutes.
3. Transfer the daikon to a large bowl and add the following: mayo, bacon, gorgonzola cheese and green onions. Stir until well combined.
4. Season with salt and black pepper to your taste. You can add some cayenne pepper for spice if you'd like. Stir again until combined.
5. Keep in an airtight container for up to 3-4 days. After 3-4 days the radishes turn sour.

Notes _____

_____

_____

_____

"Potato Salad" Two Styles With Red Radishes

"Pair this salad with my flavorful Chicharrones de Pollo
(Puerto Rican Fried Chicken)!"
—SoniaLee

asskickingwithketo —
"Keto "potato" salad made
with radishes! I added the green
onion and put some shaved
ham in it too! It's almost
potato salad. It's so damn good.
Thank you @keto_with_lee for
the recipe! So many
wonderful recipes!"

Recipe Serves

2 Servings

Ingredients - Radish -Puerto Rican Style	Amount	
Baby Red Radishes	1	cup
Mayo (low carb)	1	tbsp
Green Bell Peppers, chopped	1/4	cup
Small Red Onion, chopped	1/4	cup
Egg, hard boiled and chopped	1	----
Pitted Olives, sliced	2	tbsp
Pink Himalayan Salt to taste		----
Black Pepper to taste		----

Nutrition Facts

Servings: 2

Amount per serving

Calories	74

	% Daily Value*
Total Fat 4.6g	6%
Saturated Fat 0.7g	4%
Cholesterol 84mg	28%
Sodium 136mg	6%
Total Carbohydrate 4.8g	2%
Dietary Fiber 1.3g	5%
Total Sugars 2.7g	
Protein 3.4g	
Calcium	2%
Iron	4%
Potassium 166mg	4%

*The % Daily Value (DV) tells you how much a nutrient in a food serving contributes to a daily diet. 2,000 calorie a day is used for general nutrition advice.

Instructions – Puerto Rican Style

1. Peel the radishes and cut them into halves or quarters.
2. Boil them in salted water until they are fork tender. Not Mushy! Then drain them and set them aside to cool for 5 minutes.
3. Transfer the daikon to a large bowl and add the following: green peppers, onions, olives, mayo and eggs. Stir until well combined.
4. Season with salt and black pepper to your taste. You can add some cayenne pepper for spice if you'd like. Stir again until combined.
5. Keep in an airtight container for up to 3-4 days. After 3-4 days the radishes turn sour.

Notes

_____

_____

_____

_____

Ingredients - Radish -With a Twist	Amount	
Baby Red Radishes	1	cup
Mayo (low carb)	1	tbsp
Bacon Strips, cooked & roughly chopped	2	----
Gorgonzola Crumbles	2	tbsp
Green Onions, roughly chopped	1	tbsp

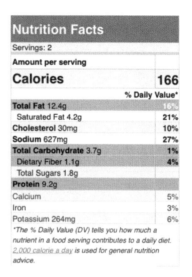

Nutrition Facts

Servings: 2

Amount per serving

Calories	166

	% Daily Value*
Total Fat 12.4g	16%
Saturated Fat 4.2g	21%
Cholesterol 30mg	10%
Sodium 627mg	27%
Total Carbohydrate 3.7g	1%
Dietary Fiber 1.1g	4%
Total Sugars 1.8g	
Protein 9.2g	
Calcium	5%
Iron	3%
Potassium 264mg	6%

*The % Daily Value (DV) tells you how much a nutrient in a food serving contributes to a daily diet. 2,000 calorie a day is used for general nutrition advice.

Instructions – A Twist

1. Peel the radishes and cut them into halves or quarters.
2. Boil them in salted water until they are fork tender. Not Mushy! Then drain them and set them aside to cool for 5 minutes.
3. Transfer the daikon to a large bowl and add the following: mayo, bacon, gorgonzola cheese and green onions. Stir until well combined.
4. Season with salt and black pepper to your taste. You can add some cayenne pepper for spice if you'd like. Stir again until combined.
5. Keep in an airtight container for up to 3-4 days. After 3-4 days the radishes turn sour.

Notes _____

_____

_____

_____

Wedge Salad
with Blue Cheese & Bacon

"This is great to pair with my brisket, fried chicken or pork chops!"
—SoniaLee

7smilesz —
"Sooooo freakin yummy!
Loved it !"

Nutrition Facts	
Servings: 4	
Amount per serving	
Calories	**391**
	% Daily Value*
Total Fat 32g	41%
Saturated Fat 9.8g	49%
Cholesterol 65mg	22%
Sodium 1302mg	57%
Total Carbohydrate 6.6g	2%
Dietary Fiber 0.9g	3%
Total Sugars 2.9g	
Protein 17.7g	
Calcium	4%
Iron	15%
Potassium 329mg	7%

*The % Daily Value (DV) tells you how much a nutrient in a
food serving contributes to a daily diet. 2,000 calorie a day is
used for general nutrition advice.

Recipe Serves

4 Servings

Ingredients	Amount	
Head of Iceberg Lettuce, Cut into quarters	1	----
Chunky Blue Cheese Dressing	8	tbsp
Bacon strips, cooked & roughly chopped	4	----
Blue Cheese Crumbles (optional)	4	tbsp
Small Red Onion, sliced really thin	1/4	----
Balsamic Glaze (drizzle drizzle)	2	tsp

Instructions

1. Cut off the stem of the head of lettuce and cut it into quarters. Each quarter is a serving.
2. Pour some chunky blue cheese dressing over the lettuce.
3. Sprinkle with blue cheese crumbles.
4. Add on some onion and bacon.
5. Finally, drizzle drizzle on some balsamic glaze! YUM!

Notes _____

_____

_____

_____

DESSERT

Blueberry Cheesecake Popsicles

"Creamy and oh so satisfying!"
—SoniaLee

Net Carbs= 1.1g

Nutrition Facts — Blueberry	
Servings: 30	
Amount per serving	
Calories	**71**
	% Daily Value*
Total Fat 6.8g	**9%**
Saturated Fat 4.3g	**21%**
Cholesterol 21mg	**7%**
Sodium 46mg	**2%**
Total Carbohydrate 1.2g	**0%**
Dietary Fiber 0.1g	**0%**
Total Sugars 0.6g	
Protein 1.2g	
Calcium	1%
Iron	1%
Potassium 26mg	1%

The % Daily Value (DV) tells you how much a nutrient in a food serving contributes to a daily diet. 2,000 calorie a day is used for general nutrition advice.

7smilesz — "The blue berry is my favorite!!!! Soo yummy!"

Recipe Serves

30 Servings

Ingredients — Blueberry	Amount	
Fresh / Frozen Blueberries	1	cup
Butter, no salt	2	tbsp
Cream Cheese	16	oz
Heavy Whipping Cream	1/2	cup
Lemon Juice	4	tbsp
Swerve (or your favorite sugar substitute)	1/2	cup
Vanilla Extract	2	tsp

Instructions

1. Combine all of the ingredients in a blender or kitchen aid. Blend or mix until smooth.
2. Pour this amazing mixture into your molds.
3. Do not completely fill to the top. You must leave room for the cover and expansion.
4. Freeze, this yummy delight for 3 hours or better yet overnight.

Notes _____

_____

_____

_____

Candied Nuts

"Enjoy and share!"
—SoniaLee

Net
Carbs=
1.3g

Recipe Serves

5 Servings of 3 Tablespoons each

Ingredients	Amount	
Sukrin Gold - Brown Sugar Substitute	1/2	cup
Water	1/2	cup
Walnuts & Almonds (raw)	1	cup
Butter	2	tbsp
Spice of your choice (optional)		----
Cayenne Pepper (optional)		----
Salt (optional)		----

Nutrition Facts

Servings: 5 - 3 Tbsp per serving

Amount per serving	
Calories	**173**

	% Daily Value*
Total Fat 16.7g	**21%**
Saturated Fat 3.7g	**19%**
Cholesterol 12mg	**4%**
Sodium 33mg	**1%**
Total Carbohydrate 3.3g	**1%**
Dietary Fiber 2g	**7%**
Total Sugars 0.5g	
Protein 5.1g	
Calcium	3%
Iron	4%
Potassium 136mg	3%

*The % Daily Value (DV) tells you how much a nutrient in a food serving contributes to a daily diet. 2,000 calorie a day is used for general nutrition advice.

Instructions

1. In a large pot over medium heat, melt the butter.
2. Add your favorite sugar substitute. For this recipe I used Sukrin Gold.
3. Once the sugar substitute has dissolved add water. I would add a little at a time until it is a loose thick mixture.
4. Stir until well combined and bring to a boil. This is where you could add any of your favorite spices such as: pumpkin, all spice, nutmeg, ground cinnamon or cayenne pepper.
5. Reduce the heat and add the nuts. Use your favorite nut but remember to adjust the macros accordingly.
6. Stir well to coat the nuts and cook for 5 minutes.
7. Move oven rack to center of the oven and pre-heat your oven to 300*F.
8. Pour the nut mixture into a colander to drain and then transfer them to a lined baking sheet. Spread and flatten the nuts as much as possible.
9. Bake for 5 minutes at 300*F.
10. Stir nuts and this is where I like to add some pink Himalayan salt. This gives it a little sweet and salty affect.
11. Bake for an additional 10-15 minutes or until golden brown.
12. Allow to cool for approximately 5 minutes prior to serving.
13. Keep these candied nuts stored in an airtight container at room temperature or you can also refrigerate them.

Notes _____

_____

_____

_____

Cheese Flan
"Flan de Queso"

"Such creamy goodness!"—**SoniaLee**

Net Carbs= 1.1g

Recipe Serves

12-16 Servings (depends on how you cut it)

Ingredients - Flan	Amoun	
Eggs, beaten	6	----
Cream Cheese	8	oz
Keto With Lee's Sugar Free Evaporated Milk	12	oz
Keto With Lee's Sugar Free Condensed Milk	14	oz
Lemon Juice	1	tsp
Vanilla Extract	1	tsp

djose92 —
"Gracias!!!!! Ive been looking like crazy for a recipe of Keto Flan!!!! Please keep this up! I love it!"

Nutrition Facts

Servings: 12

Amount per serving

Calories	152
	% Daily Value*
Total Fat 14.2g	19%
Saturated Fat 8.6g	44%
Cholesterol 124mg	41%
Sodium 95mg	4%
Total Carbohydrate 1.5g	0%
Dietary Fiber 0.4g	1%
Total Sugars 0.4g	
Protein 4.7g	
Calcium	5%
Iron	4%
Potassium 71mg	1%

*The % Daily Value (DV) tells you how much a nutrient in a food serving contributes to a daily diet. 2,000 calorie a day is used for general nutrition advice.

Instructions

1. Pre-heat the oven to 350*F.
2. Prepare your caramel and pour it into your baking dish. Be sure to swirl it around the dish to cover the bottom and set it aside.
3. In a blender co bi e all of the ingredients and blend until smooth. You might have a few lumps, but it is ok. Do not over blend.
4. Pour the yummy mixture into your baking dish over the caramel.
5. Place your baking dish onto a cookie sheet or another baking dish that is bigger. You will need to pour water into the bigger baking sheet or dish. This is called Bain de Maria or Baño de Maria, in Spanish.
6. Now bake at 350*F for 50-60 minutes or until your fork comes out clean.
7. Once done, remove the flan from the oven and remove the flan from the bain de maria. Allow to cool at room temperature.
8. Cover with plastic and transfer to the refrigerator for 3 hours, minimum. Preferably overnight.
9. Remove from refrigerator and allow to sit at least 10-15 minutes at room temperature. This allows the *sugar* to loosen a bit prior to serving.
10. With a butter knife, un-stick the sides of the flan from your baking dish.
11. Place a flat plate or serving platter over the baking dish and flip the flan over and onto the plate or platter.
12. The caramel should dance over the flan, from the top down all sides.
13. Slice and enjoy!

Please see the next page for the Caramel Recipe.
Please visit page - 84 for the Sweet & Condensed Milk Recipe.
Please visit page - 86 for the Evaporated Milk Recipe.

Notes _____

_____

_____

_____

Caramel for Flan

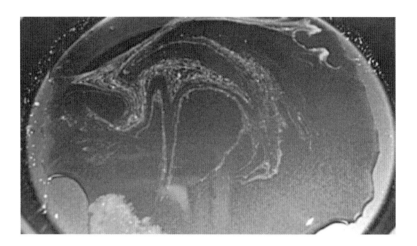

Recipe Serves

1 Serving

Ingredients	Amount	
Sukrin Gold	1/2	cup
Water	2	tbsp
Sugar Free Maple Syrup	1	tsp

Instructions

1. Add all ingredients to a sauce pan.
2. Bring to a boil.
3. Stir frequently to avoid burning or scorching.
4. Simmer until reduced and caramelized to your desired consistency.

Nutrition Facts

Servings: 1

Amount per serving

Calories	2

	% Daily Value*
Total Fat 0g	0%
Saturated Fat 0g	0%
Cholesterol 0mg	0%
Sodium 9mg	5%
Total Carbohydrate 0.6g	4%
Dietary Fiber 0g	4%
Total Sugars 0g	
Protein 0g	
Calcium	0%
Iron	0%
Potassium 0mg	0%

*The % Daily Value (DV) tells you how much a nutrient in a food serving contributes to a daily diet. 2,000 calorie a day is used for general nutrition advice.

Notes

_____

_____

_____

_____

Chocolate Cream Fruit Dip

"This is great with strawberries and raspberries!"
—SoniaLee

Nutrition Facts	
Servings: 24	
Amount per serving	
Calories	**85**
	% Daily Value*
Total Fat 8.9g	**11%**
Saturated Fat 5.3g	**27%**
Cholesterol 27mg	**9%**
Sodium 45mg	**2%**
Total Carbohydrate 2.7g	**1%**
Dietary Fiber 0.2g	**1%**
Total Sugars 0.5g	
Protein 0.1g	
Calcium	0%
Iron	1%
Potassium 0mg	0%

*The % Daily Value (DV) tells you how much a nutrient in a food serving contributes to a daily diet. 2,000 calorie a day is used for general nutrition

Net Carbs= 1.9g Without Chips

Net Carbs= 2.5g With Chips

lynntrying_keto—
"Have ya ever watched a video and wanted to lick the screen? Yep I wanted to do it with this one. Lee's chocolate cream dip. Oh my this is divine, absolutely delicious. My whole family loved it. Now I just need to hide it from them."

Recipe Serves

24 Servings (2 Tablespoons

Ingredients	Amount	
Heavy Whipping Cream	2	cup
Sugar Free Chocolate Instant Pudding Mix (1.4 oz packet)	1	— —
Sugar Free Whipped Topping	8	oz
60% Cacao Chips, finely chopped (optional)	1/4	cup

doriscamisgmailcom
—
"Delicious!!!!"

Instructions

1. Beat the heavy whipping cream and instant pudding mix in a mixer at medium speed for 2 minutes. You are more than welcome to do this part by hand. Mix only until mixture is thick. Do not over mix or else you will have chocolate butter!
2. Add the whipped topping and stir by hand until well combined. This is where you would also add the chopped chocolate chips, if you are using them.
3. Keep this dip refrigerated in an airtight container. It will be good for up to 1 week. If it lasts.

Notes _____

_____

_____

_____

Chocolate Keto-Joy Fat Bomb

"I hope you enjoy my version of the Almond Joy!"
—SoniaLee

Nutrition Facts

Servings: 14

Amount per serving	
Calories	**102**
	% Daily Value*
Total Fat 9.4g	**12%**
Saturated Fat 6.4g	32%
Cholesterol 0mg	**0%**
Sodium 1mg	**0%**
Total Carbohydrate 4.4g	**2%**
Dietary Fiber 1.1g	4%
Total Sugars 2.5g	
Protein 1.2g	
Calcium	1%
Iron	3%
Potassium 41mg	1%

*The % Daily Value (DV) tells you how much a nutrient in a food serving contributes to a daily diet. 2,000 calorie a day is used for general nutrition advice.

Net Carbs= 3.3g

Recipe Serves

12-14 pieces or more (depends on your mold)

Ingredients	Amount	
Almonds	1/2	cup
60% Cacao Chocolate Chips	1/2	cup
Organic Coconut Oil	1/4	cup
Vanilla Extract	1	tsp
Sukrin Gold (or your favorite sugar substitute)	1	tsp
Organic Un-Sweetened Coconut Flakes	1/2	cup
Coconut Extract	2	tsp

Instructions

1. In a medium microwavable bowl melt the following: chocolate chips, coconut oil and your favorite sugar substitute. Use 30 second intervals and mix after each time. You are looking for the chocolate to be melted with a smooth consistency.
2. Add the remaining ingredients and stir well until combined. This is the best place to do a taste test for sweetness. ***If you add more of something be sure to update the macros accordingly.*
3. Pour mixture into molds. If you are using silicone molds, be sure to place them on a baking sheet for stability. No need to grease the molds.
4. Freeze for 20-30 minutes,
5. Pop these goodies out of the molds and transfer them to an airtight container.
6. Keep these refrigerated or they will melt quickly due to the coconut oil.
7. When you are ready to eat these bad boys, let them sit out for at least 3-5 minutes. They will need to soften up a bit. This way you can enjoy their creaminess!

Notes _____

_____

_____

_____

Chocolate Pound Cake

"These are fabulous for a quick snack at work or home. They hit the spot!"
—SoniaLee

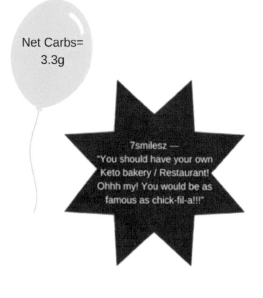

Net Carbs=
3.3g

7smilesz —
"You should have your own
Keto bakery / Restaurant!
Ohhh my! You would be as
famous as chick-fil-a!!!"

Nutrition Facts

Servings: 24

Amount per serving	
Calories	**119**

	% Daily Value*
Total Fat 11.1g	14%
Saturated Fat 5.8g	29%
Cholesterol 62mg	21%
Sodium 73mg	3%
Total Carbohydrate 3g	1%
Dietary Fiber 0.7g	3%
Total Sugars 1.3g	
Protein 3.1g	
Calcium	3%
Iron	4%
Potassium 71mg	2%

*The % Daily Value (DV) tells you how much a nutrient in a food serving contributes to a daily diet. 2,000 calorie a day is used for general nutrition advice.

Recipe Serves

24 Servings

Ingredients	Amount	
Vanilla extract	2	tsp
Almond Flour	2 1/2	cup
Butter, melted	1/2	cup
Swerve or Sukrin Gold (or your favorite sugar substitute)	2	cup
Eggs large, beaten	6	----
Baking Powder	1 1/2	tsp
Cream Cheese	8	oz
60% Cacao Chocolate Chips	1/2	cup
Un-Sweetened Cocoa Powder	3	tbs
Sour Cream	2	tbs

bxny2atl_1976—
"Those things are awesome!!"

Instructions

1. Pre-heat oven to 350*F.
2. In a small bowl combine the following ingredients: baking powder, cocoa powder and almond flour. Mix well to ensure there are no lumps and set it aside.
3. In a microwavable bowl, melt the chocolate, butter, cream cheese and sugar substitute. You are looking for a smooth consistency. I microwave this mixture in 30 second intervals, stirring between each interval, until the chocolate is softly melted, not scorched.
4. To the chocolate mixture add the following: sour cream, vanilla extract and eggs. Mix well until well combined and smooth.
5. Now you can add the dry ingredients to the wet ingredients a little at a time. Stir until well combined. Do not over mix.
6. Pour the cake batter into a greased baking dish. I like to use the muffin molds for easy portions.
7. If you are using the cupcake molds, bake for 30 minutes or until a fork inserted into the center comes out clean.
8. If using a bread pan, bake for 45-60 minutes or until a fork inserted into the center comes out clean.

Notes _____

_____

_____

_____

Coconut Candy
"Dulce de Coco"

Nutrition Facts	
Servings 48	
Amount per serving	
Calories	**128**
	% Daily Value*
Total Fat 12.6g	16%
Saturated Fat 10g	50%
Cholesterol 0mg	0%
Sodium 3mg	0%
Total Carbohydrate 1.3g	0%
Dietary Fiber 3.2g	11%
Total Sugars 1.3g	
Protein 1.3g	
Calcium	0%
Iron	0%
Potassium 2mg	0%

*The % Daily Value (DV) tells you how much a nutrient in a food serving contributes to a daily diet. 2,000 calorie a day is used for general nutrition advice.

Serrano Ricardo—
"These are the bomb,
Keto Lee!"

Recipe Serves

48 Servings

Ingredients	Amount	
Un-Sweetened Coconut Flakes	4	cup
Sukrin Gold (brown sugar substitute)	1 1/2	cup
Ginger Powder	1/2	tsp
Sugar Free Evaporated Milk (see my recipe)	1/4	cup
Vanilla Extract	1	tbsp
Coconut Extract	1	tbsp
Coconut Water / Water	1	cup

Instructions

1. **In a pot combine the shredded coconut, minced ginger, coconut water (or use just plain water) and sugar free evaporated milk.** *(Evaporated Milk recipe on page -86).*
2. Mix well and bring to a boil. Remember to stir frequently to avoid burning or scorching the milk.
3. Once boiling, add the brown sugar substitute, vanilla extract and coconut extract.
4. Simmer until all liquid evaporates.
5. Remove the pot from the burner and allow to cool for at least 10 minutes or until you can handle them enough to form them into balls. Transfer them onto a lined baking sheet to cool.
6. As they are cooling, you can carefully smash them down a little. This helps them fuse together as they cool. Or you can press them into balls again as they cool.
7. Keep these in an airtight container at room temperature.

Notes _____

_____

_____

_____

Coconut Ice Cream

""Add one tablespoon of swerve at a time while cooking adjusting to your taste and then do a quick taste test before freezing."
—SoniaLee

Net Carbs= 0.2g

NOTE:
Like any other low-carb ice cream, you must allow this ice cream to sit at room temperature for at least 5-8 minutes before digging in!

trition Facts	
rings: 6	
ount per serving	
lories	**63**
% Daily Value*	
l Fat 5.4g	7%
turated Fat 4.3g	21%
lesterol 2mg	1%
ium 2mg	0%
l Carbohydrate 1.4g	1%
tary Fiber 1.2g	4%
al Sugars 0.8g	
ein 0.4g	
ium	2%
	1%
ssium 17mg	0%

% Daily Value (DV) tells you how
h a nutrient in a food serving
ributes to a daily diet.2,000 calorie a
s used for general nutrition advice.

bibivaldes —
"So delicious!!!!...this
came out so beautifully.
Tastes like vanilla
bean coconut icecream!
So gurrrrddd"

Notes _____

_____

_____

_____

Recipe Serves

6 Servings

Ingredients	Amount	
Un-sweetened Coconut Milk (1 Can or Container)	13 1/2	oz
Swerve (or your favorite sugar substitute)	2/3	cup
Vanilla extract	2	tsp
Coconut extract	3	tbs
Heavy Whipping Cream	2	tsp
Un-sweetened organic Coconut flakes	1/4	cup

nowketo —
"Yum"

Moreno Eats —
"best keto ice cream I've seen so far on youtube! keep up the good work!"

belinda hawkins —
"U did that!!!!!! U have given new meaning to ice cream. Thank u"

Esmeralda Hernandez —
"Your recipe is honestly the only easy one"

Instructions

1. In a small pot combine the coconut milk, sweetener and coconut flakes.
2. Cook on medium-high heat for 6-10 minutes. Stir frequently and turn off burner.
3. Add vanilla extract and coconut extract. Stir until combined.
4. Now you can do a taste test for sweetness. Remember to adjust the macros if you add anything.
5. Set this aside to cool for 5-10 minutes.
6. Pour mixture into a shallow lined baking dish and freeze it for 2 hours. If you leave it for longer than 2 hours, it will become rock hard and you will not be able to blend it.
7. Break the frozen mixture into pieces and transfer it to your blender or food processor. Blend or pulse until the mixture has a shaved ice consistency. Here is where you will add the heavy whipping cream, a little bit at a time.
8. Gradually add the heavy whipping cream until you reach a soft serve ice cream texture.
9. Finally, transfer this creamy goodness to an airtight container and freeze it for 1 hour or until the mixture is firm enough to scoop.

Coconut Macaroons
"Besitos de Coco"

7smilesz —
"So delicious! They taste just like the ones with regular sugar."

Nutrition Facts

Servings: 24

Amount per serving

Calories	143
	% Daily Value*
Total Fat 13.5g	17%
Saturated Fat 10g	50%
Cholesterol 43mg	14%
Sodium 43mg	2%
Total Carbohydrate 1.5g	0%
Dietary Fiber 2.77g	10%
Total Sugars 1.3g	
Protein 2.45g	
Calcium	0%
Iron	3%
Potassium 5mg	0%

*The % Daily Value (DV) tells you how much a nutrient in a food serving contributes to a daily diet. 2,000 calorie a day is used for general nutrition advice.

Recipe Serves

24 Servings

Ingredient	Amount	
Un-Sweetened Organic Coconut Flakes	3	cup
Egg Yolks, beaten	4	----
Sukrin Gold (or your favorite brown sugar substitute)	1	cup
Butter, un-salted, melted	1/4	cup
Coconut Extract	1	tbsp
Vanilla Extract	1	tbsp
Sonia's Baking Mix	1/2	cup

Sonia's Bake Mix Recipe can be found on Page 114

Instructions

1. Pre-heat the oven to 350*F.
2. Grease a baking sheet, or you can use a silicone mat or parchment paper.
3. In a large bowl combine all of the ingredients. Mix well until a sticky dough forms.
4. Make 24 uniform balls and place them on the baking sheet.
5. Bake for 20-25 minutes or until golden brown.
6. Allow to cool for 10 minutes before serving.
7. Keep at room temperature in an airtight container.

Notes _____

_____

_____

_____

Condensed Milk

CmaxEnergi —
"This stuff is amazing.
I used it today to make
key lime pie. Next time
I'm just going to make
and eat
the filling. :)"

Miss Deb —
"This is SUPER!!"

nahid faris —
"Great recipe
thank u"

Net Carbs=
2.5g

Nutrition Facts	
Servings: 2	
Amount per serving	
Calories	**505**
	% Daily Value*
Total Fat 53.6g	69%
Saturated Fat 36.7g	**184%**
Cholesterol 122mg	41%
Sodium 42mg	**2%**
Total Carbohydrate 5.4g	**2%**
Dietary Fiber 2.9g	**10%**
Total Sugars 0.6g	
Protein 0.6g	
Calcium	16%
Iron	0%
Potassium 95mg	2%

*The % Daily Value (DV) tells you how much
a nutrient in a food serving contributes to a
daily diet. 2,000 calorie a day is used for
general nutrition advice.

Recipe Serves

2 - 8 ounce Servings	

Ingredients	Amount	
Un-Sweetened Coconut Milk (or Heavy Whipping Cream)	32	oz
Butter	8	tbsp
Stevia (or- your favorite sugar substitute)	3/4	cup
Swerve (this is to balance the aftertaste)	1	tbsp
Xanthan Gum	1/8	tsp
Vanilla Extract	1	tsp

Briggitte Rod — "...Thank you for the keto condensed milk recipe will use it on everything."

Instructions
1. In a small pot over medium-heat, melt the butter.
2. Add stevia (or use your favorite sugar substitute), coconut milk or heavy cream, vanilla extract, xanthan gum and swerve.
3. Bring the mixture to a boil. Stir often to avoid burning the cream mixture.
4. Now, reduce heat to low-heat and allow to simmer. Remember to stir frequently to avoid burning.
5. Remove from the burner once it is a thick consistency.
6. Allow to cool. This mixture will thicken even more as it cools.
7. Store in the refrigerator in an airtight container.

Note
Feel free to use the milk of your choice: almond, cashew or even heavy whipping cream. If you use different ingredients, be sure to update the nutritional facts accordingly.

Notes _____

_____

_____

_____

Evaporated Milk

"This is perfect for my keto-flan recipe, my coquito (Puerto Rican Egg Nog) for your baked goods!"
—SoniaLee

Nutrition Facts

Servings: 2	
Amount per serving	
Calories	**85**
	% Daily Value*
Total Fat 7.6g	10%
Saturated Fat 7.6g	38%
Cholesterol 0mg	0%
Sodium 0mg	0%
Total Carbohydrate 3.8g	1%
Dietary Fiber 1.9g	7%
Total Sugars 0g	
Protein 0g	
Calcium	15%
Iron	0%
Potassium 76mg	2%

*The % Daily Value (DV) tells you how much a nutrient in a food serving contributes to a daily diet. 2,000 calorie a day is used for general nutrition advice.

Net Carbs= 1.9g

Recipe Serves

2 Servings of 16 ounces each

Ingredients	Amount	
Un-Sweetened Coconut Milk	32	oz

Instructions

1. In a small pot on medium-high heat. Boil for 5 minutes.
2. Stir frequently to avoid burning the milk.
3. Reduce the heat to medium-low and allow to simmer for 25 minutes.
4. Continue stirring it frequently to avoid scorching.
5. The milk must reduce by approximately 60% to 70% from the original amount.
6. Remove the pot from the burner and allow to cool.
7. You can use this milk immediately or store it in the refrigerator in an airtight container. Enjoy!

Notes _____

_____

_____

_____

Frozen Yogurt Bark

"You can make these as popsicles to make them easier to eat!"
—SoniaLee

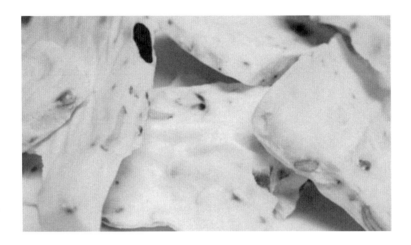

Nutrition Facts	
Servings: 30	
Amount per serving	
Calories	**29**
	% Daily Value*
Total Fat 1.5g	2%
Saturated Fat 0.6g	3%
Cholesterol 1mg	0%
Sodium 5mg	0%
Total Carbohydrate 1.8g	1%
Dietary Fiber 0.3g	1%
Total Sugars 1.3g	
Protein 2.2g	
Calcium	1%
Iron	4%
Potassium 5mg	0%

*The % Daily Value (DV) tells you how much a nutrient in a food serving contributes to a daily diet. 2,000 calorie a day is used for general nutrition advice.

Net Carbs= 1.5g

Recipe Serves

30 Servings

Ingredients	Amount	
Organic plain, whole milk greek yogurt	15	oz
Vanilla extract	1	tsp
60% cacao chocolate chips	3	tbsp
Raw almond slices	1/4	cup
Un-sweetened organic coconut flakes	2	tbsp
Chia seeds	1	tbsp
Raw pumpkin seeds	2	tbsp
Almond extract	2	tsp
Powdered Swerve -or- Your favorite sugar substitute	1	cup

Instructions

1. In a large bowl, combine all ingredients and stir until well combined.
2. Place a piece of parchment or wax paper onto a baking sheet.
3. Transfer your yogurt mixture onto the baking sheet and spread mixture as thin as you possibly can.
4. Freeze this wonderful-ness for 2-4 hours.
5. Break the frozen bark into pieces. Try to break them as evenly as possible.
6. Before chomping down on this treat, allow it to sit at room temperature for 1-2 minutes.
7. Keep frozen in an airtight container. Enjoy!

Notes
_____
_____
_____
_____

Peanut Butter Ice Cream

"Add one tablespoon of swerve at a time while cooking adjusting to your taste and then do a quick taste test before freezing."
—SoniaLee

Nutrition Facts	
Servings: 6	
Amount per serving	
Calories	**160**
	% Daily Value*
Total Fat 13.7g	18%
Saturated Fat 4.5g	22%
Cholesterol 7mg	2%
Sodium 101mg	4%
Total Carbohydrate 5.1g	2%
Dietary Fiber 1.6g	6%
Total Sugars 2.2g	
Protein 5.5g	
Calcium	2%
Iron	11%
Potassium 156mg	3%

*The % Daily Value (DV) tells you how much a nutrient in a food serving contributes to a daily diet. 2,000 calorie a day is used for general nutrition advice.

Net Carbs= 3.5g

Keto Steve — "Breaking News on all platforms : Lee has THE BEST ICE CREAM like ever!"

Alexandra Pérez — "For this easy and delicious recipe you just won a new fan. ;)"

Notes

Recipe Serves

6 Servings

Ingredients	Amount	
Un-sweetened Coconut Milk (can or container)	13 1/2	oz
Swerve (or your favorite sugar substitute)	2/3	cup
Vanilla extract	2	tsp
Heavy Whipping Cream	2	tbsp
Peanut Butter (or your favorite nut butter)	1/2	cup

chillinebony —
"thank you for this"

Instructions

1. In a small pot combine the coconut milk, sweetener and peanut butter. Make sure that the peanut butter you are using is only peanuts and salt.
2. Cook on medium-high heat for 6-10 minutes and stir frequently and turn off the burner.
3. Add the vanilla extract and stir until combined.
4. This is where you will do your taste testing for sweetness. Just remember if you add anything adjust your macros accordingly.
5. Set the mixture aside to cool for 5-10 minutes.
6. Pour mixture into a shallow lined baking dish and freeze it for 2 hours. If you leave it for longer than 2 hours, it will become rock hard and you will not be able to blend it.
7. Break the frozen mixture into pieces and transfer it to your blender or food processor. Blend or pulse until the mixture has a shaved ice consistency.
8. Gradually add the heavy whipping cream until you reach a soft serve ice cream texture.
9. Finally, transfer this creamy goodness to an airtight container and freeze it for 1 hour or until the mixture is firm enough to scoop.
10. You can add chopped peanuts on top, sugar-free chocolate syrup or chocolate chips!

Rainbow Cookies AKA: 7 Layer Cookies

"We all enjoy this special treat! Even the household non-keto'ers love this treat!"
—SoniaLee

Recipe Serves

40 Servings

Ingredients	Amount	
Swerve (or your favorite sugar substitute)	1	cup
Sugar Free Chocolate Chips (you can use less to make this layer thinner)	16	oz
Red Food Coloring Drops	20	----
Green Food Coloring Drops	10	----
Almond Paste, cut into small pieces	8	oz
Smuker's Sugar-Free preserves (raspberry or apricot) I used Apricot	12	oz
Egg Yolks, beaten	4	----
Egg Whites, beaten until foamy	4	----
Butter Sticks	2	----
Sonia's Bake Mix (see page)	2	cup
Aluminum Baking Sheets Size (12 1/4 " by 8 1/4")	3	----

Dana Pavero —
"I just made these for Easter, what a wonderful treat! Everyone loved them even the non-keto folks. Thanks!"

7smilesz—
"So freaking deliicious! One of my favorites! They don't even taste sugar-free. They are that good!""

Notes

_____

_____

_____

_____

Made in the USA
Columbia, SC
25 August 2021